RHAPSODIES
Vol.1

JAWEED AHMED

1

First published in 2019 by

Becomeshakespeare.com
Wordit Content Design & Editing Services Pvt Ltd
Unit - 26, Building A-1, Nr Wadala RTO, Wadala (East),
Mumbai 400037, India
T:+91 8080226699

This book has been funded by WORDIT ART FUND
WORDIT ART FUND helps deserving
Authors publish their work
To apply for funding, please visit us at
becomeshakespeare.com

DEDICATION

To every great poet who has scoured the earth, and left behind, modicum flames of their souls that has continued to blaze the inferno, of never dying embers of poetry.

Preface

As a poet and perfervid reader, words are never enough, and every verse of poetry is a distinct reflection of the soul of the writer.

Banded by a shared notion and strummed in one beautiful exhilaration of this book, Rhapsodies, the hearts of many writers are captured in this anthology.

This book is the very first of its kind, bringing together multinational and sensational poets under the parasol of the prestigious Face book group of Konect E-zine.

It is a collection of treasurable poetries in diverse facets of life's contemplations, sure to captivate the mind of readers with the richness of versatile emotions so profoundly portrayed.

And of course, be sure to find my contribution somewhere in there, as you immerse yourself in this inspiring and refreshing book of artistic creativity.

ACKNOWLEDGMENTS

Jaweed Ahmed
Writing is an ambrosial manna of consummate gratification, something, I am fortunate to be blessed with, and yet, a blessing is no blessing, until it spreads round, touching the lives of many a great number, if not everyone, and that has been the utmost reason for my delivery of this incredible work art, in all modesty of myself and every amazing writer who has contributed immensely to this venture, to bless the world as we have been duly blessed.

Biraj Valia
Your vision clarified this mission, in a magnitude of purposeful devotion that assembled diverse minds in a page of kindred affinity

Nirupama Jram
Dedication and patience were your unwavering doodah that never went dim, consistently, you shone your lamp and your energy never went damp.

Aafiya Siddiqui
Selflessly, you gave tirelessly in willing ways of invaluable support that is notably present in every chapter.

Tega Benny Akpodiogaga
With zeal and encouragement, you unsparingly committed yourself to the success of this noble undertaking.

Editorial Team

I am privileged to be associated with Konnect E-Zine group headed by Mr.Jaweed Ahmed. It was an honour to be invited to head the team for publishing this book of exquisite poems. Konnect E-Zine is a beautiful platform for poets to share poems and to have innovative and inspiring challenges from renowned writers from all over the globe. It was truly a pleasant experience right from deciding the title of the book, compiling the poems from different writers, proofreading, editing and finally handing over the final write-up to the publisher. This project would not have been possible without the support of Ms.Niruapma Jram, Ms.Aafiya Siddiqui and Ms.Tega Benny Akpodiogaga.
A special thanks to Mr.Jaweed Ahmed for support and beautiful designing of the book.

Biraj Valia

Editorial Team

Myself Aafiya Siddiqui, hailing from Delhi India. The writer in me is just an extension of the avid reader that I have been throughout my life. I relish writing poetry in English, Urdu and Hindi. From ghazals to nazms, from complex poetic forms to liberal free verses I have tried my hand at various genres of poetry. My learning curve took a new leap as I joined Konnect e-zine group, where I get to interact with the diversely talented literary world. "Rhapsodies" - the maiden anthology by konnect e-zine group is a cherishable milestone in my learning process. To work with eminent poets like Mr. Jaweed Ahmad, Mr. Biraj Valia, Ms. Nirupama jayram and Ms. Akpodiogaga Benedicta Oghebetega in the editorial board has been a remarkable experience. I wish continued success to the Konnect e-zine group and look forward to a mutually rewarding association in the years to follow.

Editorial Team

I am Nirupama Jayaram from the capital city of Tamil Nadu. Two years before writing became my passion. Have attempted many poetry forms. Apart from writing, cooking, and craft work are my hobbies! I'm privileged to be connected with Konnect-e-zine! Happy to be part of this book where worldwide poets are under one roof connecting the literary world through this anthology! It was truly an amazing experience of proof reading and in editorial bench, along with my co-writers, Mr. Biraj Valia, Ms. Akpodiogaga Benedicta Oghenetega, Ms.Aafiya siddiqui.

Editorial Team

I have written my name in so many places that I cannot remember, some, probably erased. But the only space that has blessed me, Tega Benny Akpodiogaga, from Nigeria, West Africa, with continuity, is my passionate reserve for writing. For me, the art of poetry is a teaching tool that has exposed me to a world where poetry flows unquenchable in Konect E-zine, a social media group on Facebook, establishing a learning rod of interaction amongst poets from all walks of life.

I am privileged to be among the editorial board, along with Mr Jaweed Ahmed, Mr. Biraj Valia, Ms. Nirupama Jram and Ms. Aafiya Siddiqui, a team of talented and soulfully dedicated individuals, to have worked on this amazing project, 'Rhapsodies', a beautiful collection of poems from multifarious poets, the first of its kind. This is but a step to the many great things we will still accomplish, and I look forward to more joint ventures of collaboration in the future, in a diligent bid to promote the literary world of poetry, sharing our souls and stories with the world.

KONECT E-ZINE

Konect E-zine Family...Connecting the Literary World.

KONECT E-ZINE

Konect E-Zine has been connecting the Literary World and aims to bring together all the writers around the world and provide a platform that enables us to come together and showcase our writing skills. We further aim to compile these literary works into Anthologies which will be made available online and also in paperback in Amazon and other platforms for those who wish to purchase. The present Anthology "Rhapsodies" Vol.1 is just the beginning and we are determined to continue our efforts by bringing next volume very soon.

On behalf of myself, Jaweed Ahmed, the editorial board, and entire administrators and members of Konect E-zine, I wish to express my heartfelt gratitude to the publication House of Becomeshakespere, for your cooperative effort in coming through with your adept and savvy expertise on this book. We are thankful, with hopeful convictions of many more workings and exploits.

SOM MAZUMDER
ADMIN

CONTENTS

Biraj Valia

Biraj Valia an entrepreneur often travels across the country for work, during these long business trips that he started writing travelogues. Learning new forms of poetry, experimenting with rhyme schemes and syllables intrigued him. Simplicity with an easy flow of expression gives his poems a unique style.

RHAPSODIES

Blows of trumpets ushers hues of twilight
Sweet flute's euphonies beseech my love near
Sway with her amidst fiddle timbres in night
Canoodling whirls gripped as piano steer
Stars twinkling stardust as beats of drums schmear
Crisscrossing steps on the lyre harp duets
Tambourine jingles set tempo intense
Night shimmering over dancers delight
Symphony preceding shame to undress
Rhapsodies enthralling lovers tonight

Biraj Valia

Nirupama Jayaram

Nirupama Jayaram is a poetess from the capital city of Tamil Nadu who writes in the pen name of njram6. In love with words she started the career in writing! Apart from writing she loves cooking and craft works!

COLOURFUL LIFE

Ghazal In English with 14 syllables per line 6 couplets. Last line signature line Nirupama- means unique!

Wrapping the sorrow, found a nameless joy, colourful life
Coded search decoded it to enjoy, colourful life

Embracing the shades of my life, I blur the scar with it
Colouring today's fate, not to annoy, colourful life

Introducing to myself, dusted were those deep bruises
Merrily dancing my joy weighed a troy, colourful life

Alongside I idolise the offerings by the life,
Making an effort to bow, oh a ploy? Colourful life

Caressing the sole heart, breathtaking is the appearance
Fondling my dear eyes, yet proved not a troy, colourful life

In the search of the meaning, let it be Nirupama
In concern of life, let me not annoy colourful life

Nirupama Jayaram

Aafiya Siddiqui

Aafiya Siddiqui is from India. She had worked as a researcher and lecturer in the field of Applied Sciences. In her leisure time, she enjoys penning down her thoughts.

AGASTOPIA

The trifling touch of your little finger
At the corner of mine
Conveying all the willingness you'd
To fulfill the unsaid promise of a lifetime
And the one you always offer,
To lead the way
Whenever the going gets tough
And I start to drown in dismay
Those annoying taps on my head
When I am all engrossed in my work
And the one that Refuse to budge
Even when I peeve with a jerk
But my favorite is how
Perfectly your fingers
Complete the gaps between mine
Reaffirming the agastopia I have
For your hand is truly divine

Aafiya Siddiqui

Tega Benny Akpodiogaga

Tega Benny Akpodiogaga is a Nigerian poet from West Africa, with a degree in Sociology and Anthropology. She's an ardent lover of God, with a likeness for reading and travelling...
She loves writing as much as she is inclined to reading. And she has written in varying formats of laconic and lengthened styles of poetries in English, with some translated in Italian that pushed deeper, into inciting the creation of her very first poetry form called 'Drip'.

Missing Diary

Wandering up and down the sun baked beach
Enjoying the twiddle of the ocean's tweed
Rattling peace in bouts of equanimity
Recycling fermented

Subsuming hues of shades and laughter
Echoing into the night
Capturing patchouli zephyrs
Tasting the warm exoticism the night has to offer

Wanderlust romance walks by
Netting hearts beside lampposts
Even the dim lights beamed in amusement
Beckoning the sparkling glows in allurement

Sleep never does come
And the lights reaffirms its prime
Waking to whispers of butterfly rays
Lavishing the warm beauty of summertime days.

Tega Benny Akpodiogaga

JAWEED AHMED
poetjaved@gmail.com
Contact: +919849096996

Jaweed Ahmed is a published author and a versatile multi lingual poet. He has written more than three thousand poems and numerous articles and essays so far. His pen name is **Javed**. He is also founder and director of six literary groups. His poems are lucid, rhythmic and deep. He is known for his unique flair and style. He hails from Hyderabad, India. His passion for poetry has been gained from his father Abbas Ali who was an Urdu poet.

SEEK

I am the drop
that holds the ocean
I am the wind
that molds the motion
I am the thought
that upholds the notion
I am the love
that extols the devotion
I am the soul
that controls the emotion
I am the pen
that denotes the passion

JAWEED AHMED

Harshad Pandit

A literary with a penchant to read and write towards promulgation of literature, for the betterment of the society.

EERIE TRANQUILITY

"Corona emerged, from where did it creep,
Leaving all mankind to smoulder and weep.
Be it a man, a motor, or a windmill,
Cometh all humanity to an eerie standstill.
Unleashing God's fury, as nature does smile,
Be it Amazon, Atlantic, Everest or Nile.
Voice of this eeriness, so very profound,
Not a soul around, and not any sound.
Spring flower has bloomed, out in the meadow,
No one to pluck, there ain't any shadow.
Confines of our homes, were ne'er so sweet,
Together we sit, to chat and to tweet.
As serenity descends, to quench my heart's fill,
A ray of hope, with moments of tranquil.
In unison we stand, to beat this virus,
Cometh together Ali, Harry and Cyrus.

Harshad Pandit

Alish Rai

Ms. Alish Rai is 20 years old, from Karachi, Pakistan. She is pursuing bachelors program in computer science from IBA Karachi.

SELFISH SON

Would that I were not see this day
My heart piece say to go away
I remember your first walk
I held your finger and made you laugh
Today I need you, not a stick
But you forget me in my grief

Would that I were a bad dream
In reality, anything is good I seen,
But you left me alone
Because of your wife hate me own
You don't know you lost demands
While getting a gold, which is bold

Would that you were know my love
You were my eyes star beloved
But I have lost my sight because of you
I wish your son will do same as you do to your father

Alish Rai

Aruna Lakra

Aruna Lakra is an Indian, from West Bengal residing in New York USA. Full time working women and a mother. Though she has done her specialization in Marketing, she has a great passion for literature. She writes to touch and soothe human souls by her simple words. A lover of multiculturalism and diversity; she enjoys listening to music and traveling. "

THE CHAOS

One small plague
Made us slave
Bowed down power
Doomed down tower
All doors closed
Humans reposed
Big and small chanting
The hymn of forgiving
Famous or the downtrodden
Earth brought them in equilibrium
Death is revolving
Wealth and pride dissolving
Manmade mountains
Drowning in wails and tears
Human touch is the curse
A memorable script in life's verse...

Aruna Lakra

Rohini Jayanti

Rohini Jayanti, loves experimenting and works hard towards achieving her goals. A Story teller and a budding writer who finds true happiness in writing short stories, articles and poems.

THE FORGIVING SELF

Melancholy visited me like a mist and surged with every expelled breath
The forgotten sorrows of a distant past
Conjured my mind as grotesque bodies under ice
And often at times left me something to remember them by
They showed an ocean of tears with million shades of gray in my soul
And flooded like the waters rushing down from a waterfall
Unheard and unseen guilt haunted me from within
Memories of the past paraded around me and
Pain remained as a veil over my mind
A numbed agony prevailed and my heart sagged with exhaustion
A quest began to defuse this bomb without causing damage to my inner self
I decided to make amends and heal and learnt to forgive myself
And moved on with the deepest love and positive remains
The disparity between my outgoing personality and inner pain started lessening
Melancholy appeared to be ephemeral
Renewed my life anew with only positivity and broke the shackles of conformity.

Rohini Jayanti

Mamu Roshid

Mamu Roshid is a budding poet from Rohingya, Myanmar. He loves to write poetry, short stories and quotes. His poems have been published in many international anthologies.

FLAWS OF THIS MAN

My outward appearance
A cute surprise
I learnt to hide
My true self in disguise

You see I use a mirror
I blur the scene
I express my fullness
Yet hide my pain from you

What I show everyone
However, the shroud is covered with meat
While inside I fight
Turbulence and disturbance

Sometimes I know I can never meet again
But outwardly I will be shinning
I love you all
Flaws of this man

Mamu Roshid

Aarti Mittal

Aarti Mittal, from Mumbai, is a bilingual poet and a teacher by profession at Rahul International School. She believes in the religion of humanity, compassion and love and staunchly follows it and believes in winning hearts more than awards.

MY BELOVED

My dear love, with your permission
Can I call you My Beloved?
The dawn today has brought the message
With its soft light, I caressed it
The chirping birds are trying to give me your
Message in their melodies
The morning that was behind the orange dawn's veil
Has bloomed with your fragrance
I am getting intoxicated with the zephyr that has touched you
Is getting your feel I have embraced it
As I close my eyes your gestures
Your valueless, valuable smile with low giggle
Tickles me beckoning me an invitation
I revert with a smile accepting it
My beloved lady
I just wish a wish
To crave for a kiss
If you permit....

Aarti mittal

Som Mazumdar

"People say that life is the thing, but I prefers reading" Like Logan Pearsall Smith said, Mr. Mazumdar Som would also like to say the same. Reading has been a part of his system since adolescence and writing followed but much later. An Ex-soldier he enjoys reading over writing and is only an occasional writer.

YOU ARE NOT POETRY

You are not poetry,
Not the emotional scribble
My old undulate diary,
Not surely my columbic drizzle
Of pent up emotions on paper,
You can never be my poetry
Not really that silly endeavor,
Caffeinated insomniac bleary.

You are definitely not the metaphor
Those shadowy sleazy by lanes
My life's futile fanatic furore
Of deceit delusions and complaints
Of the daily mundane routine,
Howsoever ardent might be the plea
Of my lazarus impudent demean
You will never end up being my poetry.

Can never allow you to be gone
To brighten my fresh new dawn
Like a danseuse's elegance
Fascinating the world as in trance
Mystic thought of a poet's mind
Someone above has been so kind
Never be my poetry my amour
My muse my rarest contour.

Som Mazumdar

Debashis Das

A young techie from Kendrapara, Odisha who is passionate about poetry and literature. He has already published articles and poems in local magazines and in online platforms as well. Apart from the poetry he is passionate about chess and have participated in state level chess tournaments also.

THE DEATHLESS

The Deathless
Swallow everything oh Sea!
Swallow both mortal and immortal, whatever exists and whatever
does not.
Just like the perpetual time swallows itself, and as the infernal
reality swallows the sublime dreams of heaven.

The night has arrived now,
See, how the prolonged waiting ends soon.
Every morsel of this world will sing the song of salvation,
Soon, the frozen glaciers will melt and the lilacs will blossom.

Every Voice will mingle with Silence,
Every beam of light will mingle with darkness.
The immortal soul will leave the mortal body alone, stranded and
will mingle with the unseen, imperceptible supreme
consciousness

How strange this night is!
The wild commotions on earth and thy impetuous heaving tides
will fall asleep again with sheer disappointment.
Soon they will realize that they are impotent and effete to wash
out the lines that my unconscious finger tips scribble on shore....

Debashis Das

Vedavati Bandyopadhyay

She believes in the religion of humanity, compassion and love and staunchly follows it and believes in winning hearts more than awards.

FUTURE

"My life is a tripartite battlefield, where my 'Present' struggles to
establish her identity amidst the carnage of my sordid 'Past'...
My 'Future' armed with hope and love
Tries to claim her ground with a blaring blast!

And Me! I'm a poor, poor soul torn in three in their everlasting
clash!
Always petulant and indecisive about whether to run a marathon
or a hundred metre dash.

When 'Future' beckons, my 'Past' glares at me, while my 'Present'
cautions me, 'hush, Baby, hush!'
I am just a pawn in their elaborate game, always an expendable, if
you must!

And I, like a caged lioness, who is complacent enough that she
forgets to roar,
Become a benign scapegoat in the game of Fates, aloof to all
chances that I ought to explore..."

Vedavati Bandyopadhyay

Atif Khurshidwani

Atif Khurshid Wani is a Kashmiri poet, reviewer and a columnist. He was born on 11th January, 1995 when everything around was frozen. Atif graduated from Kashmir University and did his masters from LPU, Punjab. Atif has become part of more than 30 national and international poetry anthologies. Currently he is working as freelancer and his poetry collection "The shattered She" is likely to be published soon.

Uneasy Dark Nights

Later in the evening
As silence came to reign
From deep dark forests
An owl hooted from its lost nest.

The wild beasts joined the tone
Muddled like kith
of one blood
Dreaming a common goal.

Children shrieked under the quilt
In these dark winter nights
with the fear gripping around
sweating like summer.

As bird hit the roof
with its half broken wings
we sighed as death
the corpse as laid beside

Atif Khurshidwani

Sihem Cherif

Sihem Cherif enjoys writing in Arabic and in English. She is from Tunisia, a North African country .She published her first book Dusk AND Dawn in India and looking forward to publishing her second book Sighs .She also writes novels and short stories.

THE SOLE RIDE

Never did you ask me to share
The ride of your prosperity and welfare
So do not resort to me in your gloom
And ask to sweep your doom
life is a large boat

Needing more than one oar
One to brush the shining rays of joy
The other to get shielded against fear
If you look for my smile and glee
watch life's book in my eyes

Leaf all the pages
Whether it bee of sad hymn or joy melody
sharing is caring
None is expected to soar with one wing
Why do not you fathom my sighs?
so I can dance with you when you sing.

Sihem Cherif

Mrs. Bidisha Sengupta (Mukherjee)

She has studied English literature, and is a poet, book reviewer and she loves everything that's creative.

LOCKED

Locked thoughts of locked hue
Locked in mind, lost in queue...
Feelings halted, thoughts paused, lost soul stagnant and stalled.
Learning lessons in lonesome state
Mind scattered as death dance with gruesome gait.
Life limping in Lucifer's Hell.
Tornado of torments tortures that which is alive -
People, animals and foliage alike.
Let the world, rotate and rotate far
Crossing planets and stars above.
Let it find a place to stay, where all are looked in the same way-
where mind and heart not divided in parts
Let's find a world where feelings are no farce.

Mrs. Bidisha Sengupta

Rose George

Rose George from Kerala is an Educator. She has contributed her articles and Poems for various anthologies. She has a passion for writing and poetry. She has organised various literary activities, language fests and published school magazines.

FREEDOM

Freedom is like the birds in the sky
It is like a smooth flowing river
We all yearn to enjoy our freedom
To choose what to do and always
Express our opinions freely to others
With courage and showing no fear
When our freedom is restricted
Anxious and worried we become
Sacrifices of our freedom fighters
Liberated us from all the struggles
From the bondage of the British
Freedom is our right to live a life
That leads to peace and happiness
When we are deprived of freedom
Punished are we, so let us break free
From these chained restraints.

Rose George

Amy Nicole Scott

Born and raised in Texas, the United States of America. I have been writing since I was eleven years old. I want to travel the world one day and write about my experiences, the food I taste, and the people I meet.

PASSION

I think it is more about
Feeling
Than a mind's eye.
To start
What feeds an interest?
About the progress

An end
Only to be chased
Not in people
Not in movement
Not in black and white
But an introduction
Of excitement
Only involving you.

This way everything after
Is trying again.

Amy Nicole Scott

Auwal Ahmed Ibrahim

He is a lecturer with Kaduna Polytechnic, Mass Communication
Department from Nigeria, a writer, a journalist and a poet.

KINDNESS

Humans are better with respect,
I wonder how you treat me with one,

It shown me that you are the best,
You are a lady full of compassion,

Everything about you is beautiful,
You are a good friend indeed,

With you I have no fears,
You give me hope and courage,

I am happy that I found an angel on earth,
You are special and a rare among all,

Being with you teaches me,
Talking with you give strength,

Here I am having a better days,
Because with you I am happy,

My prayers to you for better,
And to all the better people around you!

Auwal Ahmed Ibrahim

Ajanta Bandyopadhyay

Ajanta Bandyopadhyay, a Joint Commissioner of State Revenue
Services by profession but is a kitchen- chemist, amateur
ornithologist, and conjurer of poems by passion.

ELIXIR OF LIFE

"O' my dearest soul-mate,
I scouted your scent within a evergreen forest.
I sailed your name on the crest
of wild ocean,
I carried your flag to the highest
peak of mountain.
I searched you amongst
the fair crowd.
I tried over and over to
draw your lovely image
on the canvas open and wide.
Now that I have you within me,
myself, in my sorrows and in my joy,
I cherish every moment of life
with the elixir being sweetest of you!"

Ajanta Bandyopadhyay

Debabrata Mohanty

Former Associate Professor and his poems have been published in
two international anthologies which are Amazon's bestselling
Books -A Spark of Hope-vol2 and Break the Silence-edited by the
International author, MS Brenda Mohammed.

EUPHORIA

I know not how long I'll stay
Today or tomorrow must come the day. ..
The day won't be noisy, full of whispers,
Some will come, soon will they disperse

Have I lived long enough?
To get tired of the earthly years?
My eyes catch the sight of the azure high
As I climb the spiraling stairs.

The world is lost beyond my gaze
The sky comes floating close,
The heart gives in to the starry heaven
Forgetting the hues of the ephemeral rose.

The music chimes in my ears
I have overstayed my visit,
I have to go back home
Without losing a minute.

Debabrata Mohanty

Edache Ogwuche Moses

The poet is a Nigerian. He Obtained B.A in English and Literary Studies and NCE in English/Political Science. He has written many poems and novels; some are waiting for publication.

WEAVING FOR MY WOMEN

"I'm wealthy in words to weave
To make my weary woman well.
But, I slept so long in synagogue;
The pleasure of procrastination.

Finally, I pulled my legs in pain
From the pleasure of the pool,
And pitch my tents on white walls.
Then, she sneezed into sure safety

Our woman is weary, and needs
To see the weave of our wealth.
Let's wake to weave for her health,
Least we give to the one in wealth.

Weave now that she is wailing.
Make hay while the sun shines.
Pick the dark tread in this day,
So soon shall night fall on her.

Edache Ogwuche Moses

Rosario B. Villaluz

Rosario Villaluz is a co-author of a poetry book, titled as "Semper Fi", includes poems and verses on faith, hope and love and how these three matter in the journey of life. Along with her sworn duty for the State, she enjoys dabbling in poetry and photography and loves travelling, too.

Sweet Summer Affair

The glistening waves never cease
Racing frantically towards the shore
The calm and tender breeze
Calling passersby in a gentle 'ahoy'

Immaculate white sand tickles the bare feet
Tiny pebbles massage the parched sole
Gently calming every heart beat
Soothing balm to downtrodden soul.

Great comforting feeling
Left a weary soul in awe
A rhapsody so fulfilling
Lingers through my mind

One sweet summer affair
I will always remember.

Rosario B. Villaluz

Lukman Nurudeen

Lukman Nurudeen is a prolific writer and philosopher. He was born in OYO State, Nigeria. He is a writer of many poems, essays, short stories, novels and plays.

Fake Paradise

People of substance!
Yesterday Ones!
Where're they now?
Threnodies had accompanied them.

They live and boast of their riches
They tread on the globe
With simian feet of pompousness
Shaking down the world.
Where're they now?
Threnodies had accompanied them

Lukman Nurudeen

ASHUTOSH MEHER

ASHUTOSH MEHER is a retired SBI banker. He writes in English, Odia and Sambalpuri languages. More than twenty of his poems have been included in International anthologies so far. He has also published one Odia poem collection.

WHEN YOU CAME

Life is continuous journey that goes on and on
Sometimes pleasure and sometime full with sorrow
But time never wait nor allow you for that
It flow like a river and hit you down like an arrow.

My life was like that with journey all alone
Sorrow was only the friend along life way
I was drifting like a kite cut off from the thread
In the hand of destiny left all alone in life bay.

Things changed when you came into my life
Like some rain shower on a dry perched vacant land
Rainbow started smiling with lots of colours
And hope started singing songs with its lively band.

Life started shinning and came back on to the rails
Your efforts made me to propel in direction proper
Love lotion that you put with your soft touch around
I am feeling the effect which have driven me to prosper.

ASHUTOSH MEHER

Kishan Dahal

Kishan Dahal is a poet, writer and international human right activist, he love serving society in his own little but effective ways, he is the author of book 'waking up story's tales of tribal poet. He is from Sikkim, India."

WE SHALL OVER COME

Lazy morning!
Awkward afternoons,
Human race is all under lockdown,
Mobility seems only virtual,
Can even feel the clouds carrying messages!
Wow, is this the silence we were seeking
Or just the curse, for disobeying
Mother Nature is eternity
You see! My words are honestly speaking;
Understanding, the earth habitat
Underrated reality carry voices,
Voices that blames,
Voices that claims!
A bio warfare?
Or just an human error;
Looking for inoculation
Worried and tensed,
If this is a war,
Then, Let me fight my battle,
Where my living space is a battle field!
Staying in, is my plan
Saving world,
Ignoring the word rattle;
Spreading positivity,
Prayers and wishes
Singing the song,
Eliminating all wrong,
We shall overcome

Kishan Dahal

Jyoti Sharma

Jyoti Sharma is a research scholar and Nursing Officer for Government services in Uttar Pradesh, India. She writes poems which originates in her mind during intense imaginative moments intending to reject orthodoxy and dogmatic pursuit of Indian religion and patriarchal culture.

THE JOYLESS INDIAN BRIDE

The henna of her feet marks his threshold
Dyed in colours of heavenly-angelic joy.
His seasons in days, months and years
Turn to blossom in joys of heavenly bliss.
Every sprouted joy anew, she begets
From her body and soul tied in necklet.
Like sun that pry and peer to fill the light
She hops around and surrenders to him at night.
Braced in jewels, bangles, rings and anklet pale
She sings like cuckoo, any season it may trail.

One more year and belly-bulging round, nine months all it takes
If comes a girl, in tender curl, dark curses he then makes.
If it had been a son, a him, there may come endless joy
But being a girl, she plays with none; the chores, her only toy.
And one day, then, years ahead, henna hued on softer feet
She also parts, draped in red, to make ones only wishes meet.

Jyoti Sharma

Rakesh Chandra

He is a retired civil servant. He has authored one collection of poems Titled ""Moon is Black"" and also another collection of Hindi Poems. His English poems have found place in different Poetry Journals and News Papers' literary supplements.

LAMP POST

I'm hearing the whispering of heaven-bound
Angels by lying down in your cozy lap;
I can feel the fragrance of eternal love
By the simple touch of your hand;
You are my ever-burning lamp post of my life,
Set to illuminate my topsy-turvy journey;
Please play with my hairs with the
Feathery touch of your fingers till eternity;
I'm home far away from land of sorrows
To my cherished abode of peace and tranquility;

What is bliss I knew not, except
In the company of my loving sweetheart, where
I learnt the meaning in an exalted form;
You are my diva, my life, my love incarnate.

Rakesh Chandra

Dr Alok Kumar Ray

Dr.Ray is a bilingual poet from Odisha, India. He writes both in Odia and English. By profession he is a Senior Lecturer who teaches Political Science to undergraduate and postgraduate students.

Love of Motherland

My motherland is not only a piece of land where I live;
Like biological mother she provides selfless care,
She sings enchanting lullaby when I am in despair,
She nurtures me, she comforts me and protects me.
The unseen biblical cord that binds me with my motherland,
The sobriety of her that cherishes in me love and affection,
The enamored dreams which I crafted keeping her at the centre,
Mesmerizes me, allures me day and night in ecstatic fervor.
My thoughts take wings to flight and I glow in blissful light,
The love of my motherland is celestial, crystal like dew drops,
Sacrosanct like the Holy Scriptures.
It keeps me going, my love for her is eternal,
Invisibility is its nature and magical is its structure.

Dr Alok Kumar Ray

Zoran Radosavljvić

Radosavljević Zoran, born on **September 25, 1961** in Trebinje, Bosnia and Herzegovina. He has seven published books.

You Say Life is Beautiful

Let's swim in the waves of clouds ...
with stardust...
to shine in the firmament.
Let's fly in golden carriages non-stop...
To talk in silence...
that we are connected by fire and water ...
I dedicate this song to you ...
myself and our happy days...
now we only have that...
we look for each other in sad eyes
I will not let my darling sit in tears anymore..
Regretting his life at least for a while...
The smile on her face never to fade again...
Her name is Senada ... her name is so sweet
WHERE LOVE EXISTS, THERE IS HOPE ..

Zoran Radosavljvić

Akshaya Kumar Das

Akshaya Kumar Das is author of The Dew Drops an anthology of English poems available with Amazon/flip kart/snapdel online stores worldwide. An internationally acknowledged poet with many publications to his credit in more than twenty international & national anthologies. Recipient of many international awards for his contribution to English literature & Ambassador of Humanity from HPAW, Ghana. Sri Das regularly contributes to various literary journal & e-zines.

PLIGHT OF MIGRANT WORKERS

Corona creates panic in the world,
Humanity under severe strain on road,
Poverty stricken migrants leave for their ancestor's origin,
Running away from the pandemic situation,
From cities to homeward on walk path,
As if rejected by their habitat,
Food, shelter, water & conveyance,
Go scarce without any concrete assurance,
In a situation when self isolation is the mantra to life,
People walk long distance for safety in one sweep,
How long the body will permit?
Exhaustion & suffocation in result,
Walking long distances barefoot,
With small kids & family beating the summer heat,
Self distancing& isolation
Totally forgotten,
Children, family & luggage burden,
Life facing an acid test,
Only Survival of the fittest,
In a lockdown situation,
Life & economy facing the woes of shutdown,
Without employment & livelihood,
Where would the sudden influx lead to?
Oh! God please alight from heaven,
SOS in the crisis ridden situation

Akshaya Kumar Das

Fely Rose Nacario (Feliz Ruiz)

Dr. Feliz Ruiz is a college professor, but presently works at a government school. She writes on various subjects, though she expounds more on spirituality. She has two books published under Amazon, the Soul's Songs and Rhythm of Life.

Unity in Diversity

One world we are in diversity,
We are one family in variety
Differences we need to put aside
If service to mankind be in sight.

We've one world, one humanity
One human race in harmony
Let us pledge to come in unity
Let us work that peace be a reality.

Let love be our religion
Let peace be in words, action
Let unity be our sole vision
Let service be our mission

One system there is among creation
Food, clothing, shelter are solution
One color of blood among people of each country
With one goal, brotherhood, bring us solidarity.

Fely Rose Nacario (Feliz Ruiz)

Meenu Aggarwal

She is a teacher by profession with 37years of experience. Passionate author and poet by heart. She prefers expressing herself in English and Hindi.

VEIL MYSELF

Pandemic has rocked
My universe like a devil
I will veil myself denying
Spread n' mankind's peril.

When outer world tries
Disturbing my solitude
I want to veil myself
In a meditative attitude.

When one sarcastically
Acrid for dirty game,
I wear a veil over my
Super courageous frame

If I am betrayed by one
Of my neighborhood pal,
I play hide n' seek, a
Good garden time call.

If hawk's crooked eye,
Cuts through my flesh
Would veil myself safely
Behind mothers bless.

But whenever I commit
A mistake on my part
I will not veil myself
From my proud own self.

Meenu Aggarwal

GRACE NIVEDITA SITHARAMAN

She considers herself a Celebration; a mixture of opposites;
shooting arrows to where dreams are born. The queer keeps her
curious and curiosity keeps her wonder as a child.
Poetry is my tabernacle, my refuge."

THE GRAND COPULATION ON STONE!

Sweet dreams swell into the high seas,
Where lives the obvious, the curious,
The possibilities, the probabilities,
The glamorous disappointments of life.
I love you as you peep into my dream
As a factual head banging reality.
You are the whisper in the wind,
The caressing of passionate waves.
Naked beauty Of the Kama Sutra,
Unrequited, unspoken love stories.
The murals spell power, pride,
But no prejudice.
Of ravishing body unions and seduction.
The sculptor's obedient hormones at play.
His hands guide the chisel and hammer
Celebrating the most exciting paths
Of the grand copulation on stone.

GRACE NIVEDITA SITHARAMAN

Dr Mathura (Mavi McCoy)

Dr. Mathura @Mavi McCoy is currently pursuing M.S. in Obstetrics & Gynecology (OBGY) who has an inculcated passion for writing poems serving as a portal to rejuvenate and heal herself while a profession she loves serving as a portal to heal the humanity.

OUR PERANTIQUE BOND!

My heart will never adimpleate,
My sight will go unto nowhere whence -
Thine and mine vista will agglutinate.
Thine protracted cum eon appetence -
Shalt come true. Our bond - Perantique;
Shalt we be trace of existence?
Thy warmth; no match for thy amorevolous,
Thy tie with me hath true confluence,
Our ardors never will doth halt to be credulous;
My world dies away at your absence,
Our life never will cease to be ecstatic,
Not once can I leave you and stop to be in awe of;
Our realm - never can be made eicastic,
In no way I'll fail to admire your eyes oft.

Dr Mathura

Yahaya Qasim Oluwapelumi

Yahaya Qasim Oluwapelumi is a passionate and rising poet and novelist who has bagged few awards. He hails from Oyo state, Nigeria.

PATH OF DESTINY

I am the maker of my destiny
Through the plots of my journey
To be whom I am meant to be
And only I who possess the key

Luck might truly work my way
Situations might lead me astray
All lie in the decisions of my palms
And the hard work of my arms

I am my choices maker
My choices make my karma
My karma forms my destiny
And my density turns my reality

If success would pay me a dime
It takes my sweat and my time
The glory of my nearest future
Is on the forehead of my current adventure

If our fate totally lies with the creator
Achilles wouldn't have killed the Hector
The decision of my free will
Is what hunts me in the back still?

Albeit a hidden force pulls my strings
Carefully I choose what life brings
If from my path I do my best
Let's see how destiny handles the rest   **Yahaya Oluwapelumi**

SANGEETA KONWAR

Sangeeta Konwar is an English teacher by profession. She is from Assam, the scenic northeastern state of India and currently resides in Bangalore. She is passionate about creating magic with words and spending time with her family.

CHILDHOOD RHAPSODY

Those enchanting days of pristine childhood, filled with magical
reveries
Caressed and soaked in iridescent sunshine
Dreams as sprightly as the stars in the luminous sky
Nestles in the dreamy eyes.
Trails of hopscotch, puddles and popsicles
Tales of exonerated bonhomie and friendship.
Snapping green beans at daybreak
Grandma's fairy tales under the silvery sky.
A rhapsody so melodious-
That reverberates and echoes through the vales of the heart.
Thoughts take wings and fly to the fun-filled days
To get drenched in the shower of blissful memories-
The memories that colour the present
And nurtures the dreams of the future.

SANGEETA KONWAR

ODUJEBE OLUWOLE

He is an architect and a poetry enthusiast. He is lover of African prose and nature.

ECLIPSE ECSTASY

The Sun
Dims at eclipse
Veiled by Lady Lunar.

He burns
For her tender lips
As she wriggles closer.

The Moon
On her orbital ellipse
Flirts in sensuous manner.

She moans
In his brazen grips
Climaxing louder.

The Duet
From prying glimpse
Flew off in amorous soar

They dashed
Straight into ecstatic trips
To the paradise of lovers.

ODUJEBE OLUWOLE

Dr.Sudha Subramaniam

Dr.Sudha Subramaniam is an ardent educationist, researcher and writer. Apart from a book of poems titled 'Dawn of Creation' published by Bharatiya Vidya Bhavan, she has penned many news articles and poems for noteworthy editions.

SOULFUL

My land of dreams deserted
My daily bread gone;
With nerves of steel I live on hope
My way back home I grope.

Blood from sore legs planted on stone,
Heart drowned in uncertainty;
Will my steps reach my village?
Will I survive this carnage?

Neither food for water for intake,
Just a melancholy breeze my palate;
A masked vision meets my gaze
The looking glass is covered with haze.

Twenty-first century run amock
Now I mock your very pace;
Neither train nor plane for me to reach
This is but a humanitarian breach.

I dare to defy the rules of existence
Reaching home, I shall hug my child;
With my last breath I shall reach my goal
Mortal frame, immortal soul.

Dr.Sudha Subramaniam

Vesna Ristic

She is born in Leskovac, Serbia, where she lives and works as a preschool teacher, educator and humanist for children's rights. She has won many awards in the country and around the world. Her literary work has been published in many anthologies and journals around the world in many languages.

RHAPSODY IN BLUE

The blue of the morning heralds my awakening.
Daylight spread its wings,
She dances quietly and silently
Rhyme Rhapsody.

I break the flowers of imagination,
The rest of the blue shades of the night.
A combed space of solitude,
It kills nightmares and illusions.

I deliver all the memories
In a wonderful rhapsody of colors.
I push the boundaries for all the senses
And without resistance I pour in tenderness.

The miraculous rhythm of rhapsody
As a sign of love,
Sparkle between the lashes
And open the sense of hearing.

I hear the beep of a locomotive
Which interrupts ""Rhapsody in Blue"" for a moment.
Gershwin's shadow says:
""Don't be angry I'll play for you again. ""

Vesna Ristic

Tejaswini Patil

Trilingual poet writing in Marathi, Hindi and English. Three collections of English poems and one of Hindi poems to her credit along with one reference book. Poems anthologized in 30 anthologies in India and abroad. Awarded by Master of Creative Impulse.

ILLUSION OR DREAM

Is it an illusion or a dream?
The world is silencing the scream.
It is the Nature in its power
Man is landed from the tower.

Is it an illusion or a dream?
Egos are returned from the brim.
It's the cozy room that warms
The hearts distanced from the arms.

Tejaswini Patil

Destiny M.O. Chijioke

"My life is simple few time like the dew that spring up in the morning and dry up by the sun, that is to say my resources is for the generation coming to dry up." This is Destiny M.O. Chijioke's belief.

I Saw a New Life

Life runs like a fairytale
What we know is all that they told us
Fear is the product of our mind
Rejection incubate our heart like oxygen.
No one care about each other
We try to run faster like cheetahs
But our shadow always spot out
How vulnerable we are towards life.
Love speaks out from emotion
That bring no end of a solution
When a legacy is sold out to the street
Little filled up pocket silent our conscious.
But I saw a new life
When men are considered more than Riches
When love is express in other to save a soul not to condemn it.
When determination and courage is the way of life.
When believing work in the togetherness of heart.
When a legacy is built as a foundation.
When attention is removed from self and place in others.
When tears are only expressed not in moaning but celebration.
Has the sun lighting upon each darkness and bring hope to the
living creatures so shall our life spring up in other to bring
everlasting hope to us.
We are hope to the world stand up and take over

Destiny M.O. Chijioke

Antaryami Mishra

Antaryami Mishra is a bilingual published Poet from Odisha, India writing in both ODIA and English. He is published in a dozen of anthologies of national and international repute. He actively contributes to nearly 20 literary forums.

COVID AFFIDAVIT

Throughout the country, huge crowd of Covid
No work, wages any more, in the distant land
The hands in line on the way returning.

The traffic on roads, rails, even the sky
Crowded by people in luxury so high
'Laborers' Special' now is quite pleasing.

In Surat, Chennai, Bengaluru, Bengal
Riches visible, not we there, at all
Won't let death take our test, win and prevail.

Putting on the rags of hunger and thirst
Packing a few bundles of dear dreams lost
Homeward, handful of charcoal flickering.

Withstood floods, storms - from distance   returning
Get us chances, assess power worth watching.

Antaryami Mishra

Upendra Panda

A teacher by profession and a student of literature Mr. Upendra Kumar Panda constantly keeps interest in discussing poetries and other genres of literature. He hails from Odisha, India. Many of his poems are published in various national anthologies.

PRINCESS OF TWILIGHT

Silently steps in
Tiptoeing on blade of grass
Gathers from void the vapours
In quiet solitude of night
With her lover to converge.

Lovelorn
She waits until the dawn
When sun hugs her
With his tender light
For a moment
She glows luminously bright
And forever and ever
Does wholeheartedly merge.

Upendra Panda

Ayo Gutierrez

Ayo Gutierrez pens her art in Philippines. She is a TV personality and a professional speaker. She authored Yearnings, Evocare, and Chasing Zephyrs, among others.

Moon Shine

All of life is fragile; beauty is reductive
What are we without a desecrated battleground?
In the absence of light, we erect tall pillars of flambeau
Inside an unlit fireplace in our hearts:
They adumbrate our frail shadows on the sconces of the wall,
effaced of beauty.
Oh! How we yearn for fictions that could dim our galaxies of pain
Tears have no color, but they come: unabated, filling rivers of
abysmal deep--
Our lips are savages that stain whatever we kiss;
We leave crumbs behind, and they reincarnate to haunt us—
back.
Under the effulgent effrontery of the moon,
We simply float in a shallow bowl filled with velvety mood moss.
Evanescence of dawn; a nimbus separates,
And we await the decimation of our demons!
We rise for the hundredth time to the sound of reveille:
A bloom this perfect needs, no other blossoms to complement it.

Ayo Gutierrez

Bharati Hazarika

Bharati Hazarika is a multilingual poet from Assam, India. Her poems, stories and articles have been published in many anthologies, papers and magazines. She has been awarded Nobel Laureate Kabiguru RabindraNath Tagore Award by Arpita Foundation of Vrindavan, "AsomSahitya Award"and also ""Kabyashree Award"" for her Assamese Poetry Book "AnubhoborBoroxun"

MIST

The mist of winter
Came down softly
With a desire
To hug the Earth

The dew bathed Earth
Covered with the anchal
Of the white chador of Mist….
Lost in eagerness….

Bharati Hazarika

Manoj Sethi

Manoj Sethi is an educationist, writer and poet. He hails from Dehra Dun, India; located on the alluring foothills of Himalayas. For now, he lives in New Delhi. He is a postgraduate in Management Business with specialization in Operations Management from Symbiosis, Pune, India.

I SEE HER IN THE RAIN

Through the sprinkled droplets
On the windowpane
I see her dancing in the rain
She radiates boundless felicity
In her cherubic grace
When raindrops play mirthfully on her face

She swirls, she trots, and she hops
And plays in rhythm with the falling drops
The water runs down her ringlet hair
Clings, amuses, and besots
The felicitous shower, however
Waxes and wanes
I still see her dancing
In the rain ...in the rain"

Manoj Sethi

Shoshana Vegh

Shoshana Vegh is an Israeli poet, writer, editor and publisher, born in 1957. In 2009, she established a private publishing house and published over a hundred books for Israeli writers. She publishes articles in magazines and the Internet about Israeli poets. Her thesis was on Israeli poet Yona Wallach.

THE BURN

Into the old coal stove
I toss you
You spit fiery sparks
From my core
It is my inner world
In which you violate
My sanctity
And neither of us know
How to lower the flames
They scorch you and me
But you do not crumble and keep asking
""What can I do"?
Say, Love
I want the whole of you
Not merely the fire flaming in you
I shall lick the entirety of your skin
I quench my thirst

Come to me, Love
Come, be the solace for my body and my soul

Shoshana Vegh

Granstel Robert

Granstel Robert is an enthusiastic and fun loving person. Teacher by profession.

MY WORLD

it's not easy to pen down about you.
Because you are beyond everything
You come out with surprising qualities
You gave your flesh and blood to make my existence
You converted your blood into milk to feed me.
Yes, I was introduced to this world by you
Since the time I came into this world
You are the one who is still holding on to me.
You are the one
Who taught me to survive in any situation?
Who taught me love, caring, forgiveness and more?
I'm not at all perfect like you 'coz you are beyond perfection.
My bond with you is something more than a mother and
daughter.
Our late night chats
Our whole day shopping, cooking experiments
Our miniature fights, I will always ponder in my life...
The best painkiller in this world is to lay my head on your lap
All my worries fade away when you are with me
Nothing is comparable to your sacrifices
Yes, I can always give the treasure of love to my daughter
Like you did and try to be the best mom like you.

Granstel Robert

Mayank Dhar

Born in Kangra, Himachal Pradesh on 25th April, Mayank Dhar has been writing on issues of human interest. He is an avid food blogger and uses the pen name Culprit words across all the online platforms for writing.

MUSIC

The language so deep with often no words
Connecting souls in an invisible thread
They call it music, Oh! My friend

Chirping of birds, wild waves and dark caves
Music in their sound galore
Music in the tales of love
When that gaze ceases to go

A patter on deep dark nights of rains
When we are alone with our pains
Isn't that music of a kind?
Making us feel of someone gone

So ironical and so strange
This music accompanies the grief
Tears find their way out often finding tunes to shout
This music goes till our epitaph
Till we lie in peace marking our end.

Mayank Dhar

Bagawath Bhandari

Bagawath Bhandari is a teacher by profession and a poet by passion. He has published one of his anthologies titled "Poems with No Rhymes or Reasons" and he is on the verge of publishing one more anthology titled "The Thirty Shade of Life."

A Bird in the Woods

She chirps early in the morning,
While humans are still snoring,
She flies from blooms to trees,
In the midst of deluge of caress.

She sings akin to a nightingale,
From her nest dangling her tail,
Every petal of bloom loves her,
Eyes sparkling akin to stars.

She spreads love wherever she flies,
With her lustrous and desirous eyes,
She sings from her heavenly nest,
The rousing song at her best.

Morning gets tinted amid her voice,
In her varied hues and poise,
I listen to her lovely songs,
Sitting in my window alone.

Bagawath Bhandari

Saraswati Poswal

Saraswati Poswal is penchant in writing Poems. She is writing for many literary groups. She has written many Poems for many prompts and segments. Many of her poems are published in many anthologies. She is the author at her book 'Musing Showers.' She is working as editor for many anthologies. She writes in Punjabi, English and Hindi.

SHADES OF LIFE

Life carries the distinct shades with perceptions of distinct minds.
Flowers of various colours bloom.
Sometimes only dark and sometimes glooms.
Some are faded and dusky brooms.
Some days are vibrant like the violet hues
Some are milky white...
Bestowing peace to you.
Some are green like hues.
Some are golden like the rays of sun.
Crunchy and adorned.
Some leave the silver effects.
Grey shades for some.
Some are redeemed like a rose.
Some blush in pink and pose.
Perceptions, what we adore.
Those shades we wore.
Sometimes nights are chosen to be bright
Sometimes days become beckoning dark like night.
This is norm of every life.

Saraswati Poswal

PRANAB BEHERA

Pranab Behera, hailing from Kalahandi in Odisha, is serving as a Reader in English at Women's College, Junagarh.

FLIMSY BLACK CURTAIN

At twilight we all loll in the veil of night,
A flimsy black curtain slowly shrouds vision,
The moon finds her caged in the dungeon of clouds,
Owls hoot and bats screech to drag the shadow of darkness
To its fearful depth where stillness trills its own symphony,
Our trifling drudgeries are thrown into some hinterland,
In the brace of rest and repose,
We sneak into an unknown dreamland,
Angels and fairies tread on soft
Carrying and scattering His message of peace and bliss,
Blessed and soothed, we sleep the night away
As stars and galaxies remain watchful above
With their ceaseless glinting eyes,
They adorn our night with their cosmic lilting lullaby,
But with darkness dispersing into orange bright
They somehow fade into a renewed day.

PRANAB BEHERA

Jyotirmaya Thakur

Jyotirmaya Thakur (retired vice Principal) is the author of 21 books, Multi - genre award winning poet, book reviewer, columnist, editor, literary & social researcher. World Poet Laureate, Living legend of 21st century, Peace Icon and HPAW Ambassador of Humanity and Universal Ambassador of Art and culture by WUAC ,Bolivia.

TAKE A MOMENT

Take a moment to slow down,
Putting all the worries behind,
Take in the beauty all around,
Let it relax and calm your mind.

Watch the golden glow promise,
Of rising morning with the Sun,
Embrace your peaceful aura,
With the break of glowing dawn.

Listen to nifty tunes of soft caress,
Of gently moving breeze in trees,
Enjoy the luxury of lovely scenes,
Graceful wings in flights with tweets.

Spare a thought in a still moment,
Every day, at least once in a while,
Take in beauty of sights and sound,
Look around and take time to smile.

Jyotirmaya Thakur

Suzette Portes San José

A widow and a retired scholar. An international contributor of poetry and arts. She paints the visual of every poem that she writes. Also a founder of a charity "Children Art Basics".

THERE IS TOMORROW

I watched the sun going down at twilight
The color deeming slowly out of my sight
Darkness hovering skies in a silent night
With passing hours waiting for sunlight

I felt the wind touching my skin...so cold
Wrapping the heart and soul that I behold
With this journey of life to tell and be told
In riddles and puzzles in a hundredfold

Eyes may fall in slumber for thousands of day
Frozen amidst the blooming sunflowers to stay
Towing the tears as the morning dewdrops lay
On velvety soft petals under the suns colorful ray

Awakened in a morning of fulfilling brightness
Smiles reborn without the blues of lonesomeness
Dares another day to trail once more in the vastness
The trodden and the untrodden in life's wilderness.

Suzette Portes San José

Aida G. Roque

A Sped Teacher and a bilingual poet/ writer hailed in the Philippine and presently residing in the USA. A self-published author of 4 children's books and 3 Collections of her Poetry books. An international poet and recipient of numerous global awards and co-authored anthology with poets, worldwide.

A MELLIFLUOUS ANGEL WITH GOSSAMER WINGS

I heard a mellifluous voice, and I rejoice,
An angelic choir in harmonious wonder.
Twirling in gossamer, veil in wander.
Gold dust drizzled from the sky asunder,
A mellifluous angel, in gossamer wings,
Rendered.

It floats in thin air, like a bride walking
Down the aisle with flair. Like a fairy in
White gossamer wings and continued
To sing a mellifluous verse, a mystery
Abound. Swinging and spreading joyful
Greetings, sending and wishing everyone,
A world of healing.

Aida G. Roque

Yazda Ashrafi

Yazda Ashrafi hails from Hazaribagh, an MBA graduate from Hazaribag India Presently working as principal of a school.

CORONA VIRUS

A small virus, popped up to rectify the world, it substantiated us
Plants and animals are masters of earth, we are guest
For worship pure heart is essential not posh temple or mosque
Home is best place to delight not the plaza or square
Salam, Namaste are best greetings, hand shaking is misdemeanor
Carrying sanitizer is essential not the perfumes
Media should debate in science political news not required
In matter of public health, Asian models is superior
Bride and groom are important in marriage not the guest
Badge of foreign return is suspect of spreading virus
Washing hand wearing mask are like oxygen to survive

Yazda Ashrafi

Sandeep Kumar

He believes in his inner voice and uses a pen name Zinda dil sandeep. Banker by profession and believes writing is the best way to enrich life and soul. Smiling and spreading smiles in all situations is his motto of life.

In the End

In the end when life comes be under seize.
Often we see emotions on the verge of decrease.
Hold my hand and walk me through.
Giving it all away. Happiness without any clue.

Mesmerized with joy of surviving at last.
Times gonna change someday slower than fast.
Eternity a myth for the ones in the race.
Oh lord! Give me the strength for smiles in my face.

Never acquitted nor ever blamed.
I am a fire which can never be tamed.
Writing thoughts open hearted is all I do.
Don't look for me there, I am always inside you.

Sandeep Kumar

Bishakha Moitra

A stay at home mom, Bishakha is an artist by passion. Writing, to her, is expressing her emotions, thoughts and opinions in a way that others can feel the connect. She uses 'a gypsy soul' as pen name for writing. You can read her writings and follow her page on Instagram.

PROPOSAL OF LOVE

"That enchanting smile of yours
Persuades me to cross the distances between us
The sadness in those deep oceanic eyes
Urges me to solve the differences between us
The pearl drops on your cheeks
Makes me go completely weak on my knees
The waves of your boundless tresses
Impels me to flow in the sea of passion and bliss
These blooming buds of your rosy lips
Lures me to drink the juicy nectar like a bee from the flower sips
You and everything about you, are making me fall hard for you
In my every thought it's you and only you
I breathe your breath, I dream your dream
I want to make love to you till you in ecstasy, scream
My passion for you is driving me insane
I could forget everything,
Only my eternal love for you will forever remain.

Bishakha Moitra

S Gayathri Vijayaragavan

Born on 4th October 1992 in Tamilnadu. Gayathri is an engineer. Her enthusiasm, willingness to learn and experiment gives her the push for an amusing, enthralling and flabbergasted journey to start every day.

WAIT IS SO LONG

Await the stars to shimmer.
Bewitching the silhouette from far.
Reverie the night to become dimmer.

Where the dreams leave the scar.
A pause which changed the world around.
Questioning the sanctity of life from afar.

Verses still reminiscent those sounds.
Fissuring the camouflaged vision.
Squeaking everybody to astound.

Moments weave the life's precision.
Delineating the quill to whisper a song.
Sky bewilder the incision.

Agitating the chaos to diminish all along.
Soul pave the solidarity to enshrine,
Whenever the wait is so long.

S Gayathri Vijayaragavan

Ranjana Bansal

She has great passion for writing. She has inked number of poetry,
blogs, articles, short stories in English & Hindi for different
platforms. Her creations have got published in different
anthologies. She is a school Principal in Rewa (M.P.)

ODE TO THE PEN

My darling pen!
You are my intimate friend,
Nothing is hidden from you
Each secret I reveal to you,
Safely them you always keep
Confidential, you intelligently unveil,
You are a smart juggler
First you play with the depth of words,
Later you share them with blank paper
So aptly and proper,
You trick, next ink in supporting words
Thence you are loved by bards,
Openly you engrave firm and blunt
Your creation may occasionally hurt,
Yet I am proud of your ingenious
No matter sometimes it causes stress,
Regardless you are criticized by others
O mighty Pen! You echo my 'JAZBAT' to this emotionless world.

Ranjana Bansal

Ency Bearis

Ency Bearis is a Registered Nurse by profession, being inclined to poetry, he is a Poet and Author. He had published several poetry books, which are available on www.amazon.com. He was born and raised in the Philippines, now lived with his wife and two children in Las Vegas, Nevada, USA.

SOULS JEREMIAD

Within silence site, voices in cadence
Something the soul's sigh of frustration
Themselves in hopeless ambience
At the inner core of destitute section

Sighs maybe from persons in whys
Be heard as pitiful tedious clamor
For it's in barren life they realize
Being thirsty within life like summer

Making the family more cramped
Likely with feel of dehydration
Shriveled like dry leaves, parched
Being poor, languishing situation

With hovering joy in twilight time
Floating over their heads dream future
But can't be achieved, needy in grime
Soul's jeremiad about their culture.

Ency Bearis

Dr. AMIYA ROUT

Dr. Amiya rout had retired as a Reader in Sociology. Two poetry collections, two novels in Odia and four translated novels to his credit.

THE SONG

On this earth moment, did I come into a being?
Since then, the song of renunciation have I been singing
Like water drops in the flowing stream;
Life after life, for that is increasing my scream;
Passing through states: stone, plant, animal
And man...with desires help;
Tired of voyage, am I to get a divine shape.

Dr. AMIYA ROUT

Gulnaaz Saif

Gulnaaz Saif is a poetess by passion, who aspires to inspire before she expires.

FUNERAL

Powerless and feeble on my bed I lay,
My once sturdy, brawny muscles shall soon decay,
"Every soul has its given date," they say,
As soon as the Angel Of death snatches my breath away.

The concrete floor replaces my comfy bed,
'Corpse' is what they call me, as soon as I am dead,
They lay me here motionless and still,
Not blind, I watch everything, just my body lying chill.

Some shriek and screech, some snivel and sob,
Tear shed from the eyes of the gathered mob,
A few serious rest just pretend,
On my funeral have come, both my foe and friend.

The time flies and they wrap me in the clean shroud,
I realize to dust we shall return, me and my proud,
They put me in the dark coffin and enter the graveyard gate,
Leave me in the darkness of the sepulcher where I meet my
eternal fate.

Gulnaaz Saif

Nitesh Sharma

Nitesh Sharma (1987) is a poet and fiction writer from north-western part of India. His poems are deeply draped in saccharine rhyme scheme and felicity of ideas reflecting an undertone of aesthetic quality. The poem expresses a medieval happening in witty anagrams. His pen name is Teshin Armash.

I SAW IN WOODS WHEN I WAS A CHILD

I saw in woods when I was a child,
Two maids with the eyes too severe wild.
The eyes they see through, O eerie gleam!
Could take any mate in their team.
Lots of men, alas, had lost their slot of wiser sane,
To say all Man: hard, lean or round, in lovely dark woods' lane.

To save the slot, like many lots, from being it there lost,
Behind the thickest, thickset of thickets, to me I thus then posed
And saw them live in the veil of sleep, weird wider trees around,
In the time when forest does foster the softer soothing sound.

As silent as moves the cat, not voicing a note to listen,
As silent as crawls the sun, to lend the world to glisten,
I crept to north, closer than close, and picked a pointed thorn
Gouged it in, green blood gushed out from where vile-evil was born.

Since then the day, the tribe of men, state with swollen taste:
How sainted boy saved medieval life from being stained in waste.

Teshin Armash

Neetu Chhabra

Neetu Chhabra is a native of Sukkur, Pakistan. She pursuing her Masters in English Literature. Writing poetry and sketching are her passions.

MY GRANDFATHER

My grandfather made me laugh
I enjoyed it and played with him a lot
He told me motivational story
Which fulfilled my heart with glory".

""He had silver hair and golden sticks
Wisdom, knowledge and many tricks
He walked out the door beside me
That was the precious time for me"".

"But the fact that He was no longer there
The pain which I bear, I can't express here
Those special memories were unforgettable
Which bring smile on my face unbelievable".

"He lives in my heart, and his voice I feel
I closed my eyes but my pain doesn't heal
If you have a grandfather, so love him
Spend your more time, and cherish him.

Neetu Chhabra

Christian Duarte

A 21 year old graduate with Major in English

Un Riddling the Metaphors of Us

You're a book,
I'm a cat.

You're a coffee,
I'm a kite.

You're a star,
I'm a pair of shoes.

You're a pen,
I'm a bird.

You're an ocean,
I'm an apple.

And yet, here I am,
Still trying to make sense of us.

Wondering, figuring out
How & when can we be perfect for each other?

Christian Duarte

Ratikanta Samal

He is a teacher and a bi-lingual poet as well. He has published six poetry books-two in Odia and four in English. Many of his poems have been published in different anthologies, magazines, e-magazines and Journals.

The Grass of Parnassus

Very pretty and elegant you look
Appear During mid-summer days,
And dotted around the low lands
The earth brings the starry skies.

A beautiful British white look
Dances with north polar wind,
Smile in little petals spreads and
Infatuates all heart and mind.

The sun removes the snow curtain
And breaking hibernation on earth,
The renascent grass of Parnassus
With five White petals takes birth.

Boosts the glamour of the low land
Patches of white cloud in the green,
Live wild, not withstanding decorate
The grassy lands that the hearts win.

Angel like beautiful British white lady
Captures the grandeur of land and feels,
What Hughes assemble in his portrait
Elegance wins and everyone appeals.

Ratikanta Samal

Naheed Akhtar

Naheed Akthar, an Indian poet, holds a master's degree in English literature. She is a lecturer by profession, a poet and writer. She has a rich taste for Classical and Romantic poetry, however, a sense of originality is vividly seen in her style of writing.

Her poems have been published in various anthologies. And have also been published in her own book of poetry, "Phantasms of My Heart."

She is a prolific writer, and continues to write during her free time, away from college. She looks forward to publish more of her works in magazines and periodicals. She lives in Hyderabad with her family.

DESPERATE!

If a million steps away
I am to reach
I want you to come forward-
For I wish to see how desperate you are!
But, stop a step before,
In that one step
I shall show you
How a million times more desperate I am...!!!
To recognise in reality
The perfumes I smell in my dreams
The onyx eyes staring me
The light brown hair I caress softly
Engrossing fingers gently...
The sharply shaped brows
The thick eyelashes
Lethal with sleep,
Half open half closed,
How I get intoxicated
For days, unless
Heart gets again
Restless, feeling ignored

Usually ignored!

Naheed Akhtar

Bharati Nayak

She is a bilingual poet and translator from Bhubaneswar, India. She has published three poetry collections and co-authored in three books and edited one book Radical Rhythm Vol-III written by members of Cosmic Crew (a group of women poets).

MOON

Moon!
When did we meet first?
Was it at my birth?
Or was it
When I was planted in mother's womb
In a night lit by you
And saw you through my mother's eyes,
Who dreamt a child like you
Lovely, beautiful and tender?
But our relationship is for ages
Since you circled the Mother earth
Born out of a chunk
From earth's womb!
My mother introduced you as 'Jahna Mamu'
The Moon uncle
And I always desired to go near you
And when this earth's scientists went to you
In flesh and blood
You remained no more a distant mystery
In their camera they captured images
That are rough, sandy, rocky
Even there are no greeneries
Like our earth
Nor are there any birds or flowers
But I wonder
In spite of no life
How you look beautiful
From this distance!

Bharati Nayak

ABOUT THE AUTHOR

Jaweed Ahmed

Jaweed Ahmed has pursued M.Sc. (Mathematics), M.Sc. (Physics), M.Sc. (Psychology), M.A. (English), PGDCA (Computer Science), B.Ed. He is a multi lingual published author, a versatile poet and a wonderful writer and an enthusiastic educationist from Hyderabad who has written more than three thousand poems, numerous articles, essays and stories in English, Hindi and Urdu so far. Many of his works have been published in National and International Magazines, Anthologies and Newspapers. He has published his own books **"Peerless Pearls"** and **"Precious Jades"**. His poems are Sufi in nature, and his style so simple yet his thoughts are so intense and deep. He is known for his lucid and unique style. He has learnt all these from his father Mr. Abbas Ali who was an Urdu poet. He used to attend Urdu Poetry Symposiums in his boyhood days along with his parents. The poet possesses a sensitive heart which listens when nature talks to man in myriad voices, but he is very clear that all these messages are for those who have a mind which can articulate its messages and then obey them. His poetry springs like a scintillating stream and flows like a delightful dream. As a master craftsman he has no dearth of themes. He burns midnight oil to script his verses in stunning splendor. There is unusual mystical insight and charm characterizing his poetry. His enormous enthusiasm towards literature is an endearingly ennobling trait. He is also Founder of many Literary Groups. The present anthology **"RHAPSODIES" Vol.1** is an attempt to promote literature and give a glimpse of his enthusiasm towards it.